First World War
and Army of Occupation
War Diary
France, Belgium and Germany

51 DIVISION
154 Infantry Brigade
King's (Liverpool Regiment)
8th Battalion
1 May 1915 - 31 December 1915

WO95/2887/1

The Naval & Military Press Ltd
www.nmarchive.com
Published in association with The National Archives

Published by

The Naval & Military Press Ltd

Unit 10 Ridgewood Industrial Park,

Uckfield, East Sussex,

TN22 5QE England

Tel: +44 (0) 1825 749494

www.naval-military-press.com

www.nmarchive.com

This diary has been reprinted in facsimile from the original. Any imperfections are inevitably reproduced and the quality may fall short of modern type and cartographic standards.

© **Crown Copyright**
Images reproduced by permission of The National Archives, London, England, 2015.

Contents

Document type	Place/Title	Date From	Date To
Heading	WO95/2887/1 8 Battalion King's Liverpool Regiment		
Heading	51st Division 154th Infy Bde 8th Bn King's L'pool 1915 May-Dec 1915		
Heading	War Diary 1/8th (Irish) Bn King's Liverpool Regiment Period: 1st To 31st May 1915 Inclusive Vol I		
War Diary	Becyord	01/05/1915	03/05/1915
War Diary	Folkestone	03/05/1915	03/05/1915
War Diary	Boulogne	04/05/1915	04/05/1915
War Diary	Pont De Briques	04/05/1915	04/05/1915
War Diary	Fontes	05/05/1915	07/05/1915
War Diary	St Floris	07/05/1915	14/05/1915
War Diary	Merris	15/05/1915	18/05/1915
War Diary	La Gorgue	19/05/1915	20/05/1915
War Diary	Locon	21/05/1915	21/05/1915
War Diary	Le Casan	22/05/1915	25/05/1915
War Diary	Rue Du Bois	26/05/1915	28/05/1915
War Diary	Trenches & Richebourg L'Avoue	29/05/1915	29/05/1915
War Diary	Richebourg L'Avoue	29/05/1915	31/05/1915
Heading	War Diary Of 1/8th (Irish) Bttn. The King's (Liverpool Regt.) From 1st June 1915 To 30th June 1915 Vol II		
War Diary	Richebourg L'Avoue France	01/06/1915	02/06/1915
War Diary	Le Cornet Malo	03/06/1915	06/06/1915
War Diary	Le Touret	07/06/1915	09/06/1915
War Diary	La Quinque Rue (Trenches)	10/06/1915	12/06/1915
War Diary	Pacaut	13/06/1915	14/06/1915
War Diary	Le Touret (Trenches)	15/06/1915	15/06/1915
War Diary	La Quinque Rue (Trenches)	16/06/1915	17/06/1915
War Diary	Pacaut Wood	18/06/1915	22/06/1915
War Diary	Hinges	23/06/1915	24/06/1915
War Diary	Estaires	25/06/1915	25/06/1915
War Diary	Laventie (Trenches)	26/06/1915	28/06/1915
War Diary	Laventie	29/06/1915	30/06/1915
Heading	War Diary Of 1/8th (Irish) Bn The King's (Liverpool Regt.) 1st July 1915 To 31st July 1915 Vol III		
War Diary	Laventie	01/07/1915	09/07/1915
War Diary	Picantin	10/07/1915	15/07/1915
War Diary	Le Nouveau Monde	16/07/1915	23/07/1915
War Diary	Neuf Berquin (Near)	24/07/1915	24/07/1915
War Diary	Neuf Berquin	25/07/1915	27/07/1915
War Diary	Corbie	28/07/1915	28/07/1915
War Diary	La Neuville	29/07/1915	30/07/1915
War Diary	Bouzincourt	31/07/1915	31/07/1915
Heading	War Diary Of 1/8 Kings (Liverpool Regt) August 1915 Vol IV		
War Diary	Aveluy	01/08/1915	14/08/1915
War Diary	Senlis	15/08/1915	21/08/1915
War Diary	Aveluy	22/08/1915	31/08/1915
Heading	War Diary 1/8 Kings (Liverpool Regt) September 1915 Vol V		
War Diary	Aveluy	01/09/1915	11/09/1915

War Diary	Martinsart	12/09/1915	18/09/1915
War Diary	Aveluy	19/09/1915	21/09/1915
War Diary	Millencourt	22/09/1915	26/09/1915
War Diary	Aveluy	27/09/1915	30/09/1915
Heading	War Diary Of 1/8th (Irish) Battalion The King's (L'pool Regt) From 1st October 1915 To 31st October 1915 Vol VI		
Heading	1/8th (Irish) Bn The Kings (L.pool Regt.) War Diary From Oct 1st To Oct 31st 1915		
War Diary	Aveluy	01/10/1915	31/10/1915
Heading	War Diary Of 1/8th (Irish) Battalion The King's (L'pool Regt) From 1st To 30th November 1915 Vol VII		
War Diary	Aveluy	01/11/1915	07/11/1915
War Diary	Millencourt	08/11/1915	16/11/1915
War Diary	Authuille	17/11/1915	28/11/1915
War Diary	Millencourt	29/11/1915	30/11/1915
Heading	War Diary Of 1/8th (Irish) Battalion The King's (L'pool Regt.) From 1st December 1915 To 31st December 1915 Vol VIII		
War Diary	Millencourt	01/12/1915	05/12/1915
War Diary	Aveluy	06/12/1915	16/12/1915
War Diary	Millencourt	17/12/1915	20/12/1915
War Diary	Authville	21/12/1915	31/12/1915

WO95/2887/1

8 Battalion King's Liverpool Regiment

51ST DIVISION
154TH INFY BDE

1-8TH BN KING'S L'POOL
1915 MAY - DEC 1915

To 55 DIV 164 BDE

Box 2887

Badly written — *Pte.*

51st Division

Confidential.   121/5617

War Diary

1/8th (Irish) Bn. King's Liverpool Regiment

Period: 1st to 31st May 1915 inclusive

Vol I.

WAR DIARY or INTELLIGENCE SUMMARY

Army Form C. 2118.

(Erase heading not required.)

Hour, Date, Place	Summary of Events and Information	Remarks and references to Appendices
1915		
6.30pm 1st Mo Aedgd Oural		
9 " " "	Camp Oural	
12 mn " "	Passed 4 advance party (3 Officers 104 other ranks) for ruen.	
8pm " "	Remds. of advance party proceed crossing town	
	3 Officers 104 other ranks proceed over souterstrops and Havre.	
	JD. Clerk Oural Outrich Oural	
2nd Mo Aedgd "		
2.04 " "		

Army Form C. 2118.

WAR DIARY
INTELLIGENCE SUMMARY
(Erase heading not required.)

Instructions regarding War Diaries and Intelligence Summaries are contained in F. S. Regs., Part II. and the Staff Manual respectively. Title pages will be prepared in manuscript.

No. 2

Hour, Date, Place	Summary of Events and Information	Remarks and references to Appendices

1915

3.40 p 3rd May Redhill — Move by train to FOLKESTONE.

9.30 p " FOLKESTONE. Boat to BOULOGNE, Camp at ESTRAHOVE. JB

12.10 p 4th May BOULOGNE. Move from BOULOGNE to PONT DE BRIGUES Railway Station.

1.50 p " PONT DE BRIGUES. Meet. Advance Party who came via SOUTHAMPTON and HAVRE and proceed by train via CALAIS — ST OMER — HAZEBROUCK to BERGUETTE. Disentrain and march to FONTES and then billet — most from Lewisham and Jones — very many boys.
JB Battalion rests.

5th May — FONTES   "   "   Battalion Parade.
2.30 p   "   JB

WAR DIARY

INTELLIGENCE SUMMARY
(Erase heading not required.)

Army Form C. 2118.

3

Hour, Date, Place	Summary of Events and Information	Remarks and references to Appendices
1/5/15 FONTES		
6.30 am	ROLL CALL	
9 am	Battalion Paraded for Brigade entertainment	2
9.30 am	Brigade not moved cancelled order received to be prepared to move to front billets at 5 pm.	
5 pm	Proceeded on march route given Brigade at LILLERS — from there via BUSNES to ST FLORIS — then billeted not later than 5/5/15	
3.30 p 1/5/15 ST FLORIS	Parade of Battalion inspected by right about commanding Officers and Adjutant to Colonne men-CO's given orders of welcome from Brigade.	
9.30 p		

WAR DIARY
INTELLIGENCE SUMMARY
(Erase heading not required.)

Army Form C. 2118.

Hour, Date, Place	Summary of Events and Information	Remarks and references to Appendices
1918		
8th May. St Floris.	In reserve at St Floris	
9th May. St Floris	Church Parade. Battalion in reserve.	
10th May St Floris	Battalion in state of readiness.	
11th May St Floris	Battalion in state of readiness. Coys training.	
12th May St Floris.	Coys Training. 3rd Highland Infantry Brigade in Relief 154 Infantry Brigade.	
13th May St Floris	Coys Training.	
14th May St Floris 8.30am	Orders received to be prepared to move at 8.30am. Moved with Brigade via Calonne-sur-Lys — Merville — La Rianne — Neuf Berquin — Vieux Berquin — Merris and then Billet.	

WAR DIARY

INTELLIGENCE SUMMARY

Army Form C. 2118.

Hour, Date, Place	Summary of Events and Information	Remarks and references to Appendices
1915		
2.30 15th May MERRIS	Coys. arrival — Inspection by Commands. Major Smyth far Major J Coughlan and Adjutant; Command C Coy E. Command D Coy; Capt. Williamson B Coy; Command C Coy — Capt. Brown for D. & Capt H. Colonel Parade	
16 May MERRIS		
6.55pm "	Orders received to be prepared to move out 2 hours notice	
17 4am MERRIS	Battalion in a state of readiness	
9am 18th May MERRIS	Proceed to Surgical Menil via Vieux Berquin — Neuf Berquin to La Gorgue arrive 3pm	
19 " " " La Gorgue	Present Battalion at La Gorgue	
9am 20th May La Gorgue	Proceed to Surgical March via Vieille Chapelle to Locon	

WAR DIARY
or
INTELLIGENCE SUMMARY
(Erase heading not required.)

Army Form C. 2118.

6

Hour, Date, Place	Summary of Events and Information	Remarks and references to Appendices
1915		
21st May LOCON	Mine shell 6. East of Lawe River – Locon. Lieut Downes appointed Instructor Musfre Casan 152 Inf Bde	
22 May Le Casan	Battalion now Casan – Corps Reserve	
23 May Le Casan	Church Parade	
24 May Le Casan	Corps Reserve	
5.30 25 May Le Casan	Received by rail. Moved to send Pte 80 L'EPINETTE Relieved early, relieved to wood east of Rue du Bois and rel'd in Battalion in Brigade Reserve. 1/4 R Lanc Regt Batt left. 1/5 N Lanc Regt Batt right.	
26 May Rue du Bois	Battalion in Brigade Reserve	
27 May Rue du Bois	Battalion in Brigade Reserve Capt J. Ellison and 2/Lt G visited trench of 2 Batt in Bois Grenier and returned – one man killed 10 kind Cpl wounded in flag's unofficial leave Lieut J. Allen	

WAR DIARY / INTELLIGENCE SUMMARY

Army Form C. 2118.

Hour, Date, Place	Summary of Events and Information	Remarks and references to Appendices
1915		
8 pm 28th May RUE DU BOIS	Leave trenches — relieved 1/4 King's Own (Royal Lancaster Regt) at north end between RUE DU BOIS on north end LA QUINQUE RUE on SOUTH (firing line from G 9 to known as 22nd West Pno)	
29th May Trenches RICHEBOURG L'AVOUÉ	2.20 Occupied trench — attacked some hrs. for artillery bombardment — chiefs kpt rifle and small arms shrapnel. Enemy right over firing head (about 150 yards in front of old firing trench) commenced	
30th May RICHEBOURG L'AVOUÉ	2.10 As on 29th May — Enemy rifle on firing line improved — all communication trenches improved. Casualties in day time 2 men killed 5 wounded	

1247 W 3299 200,000 (E) 8/14 J.B.C. & A. Forms/C. 2118/11.

WAR DIARY
INTELLIGENCE SUMMARY
(Erase heading not required.)

Army Form C. 2118.

Instructions regarding War Diaries and Intelligence Summaries are contained in F. S. Regs., Part II. and the Staff Manual respectively. Title pages will be prepared in manuscript.

8

Hour, Date, Place	Summary of Events and Information	Remarks and references to Appendices
1915 31st May RICHEBOURG L'AVOUE	In trenches as above - attention given to to strengthening entrenchment. Casualties. 3 men wounded.	

51st Division   2 W. 9 sheets.

"Confidential"   121/6023

War Diary

of

1/8th (Irish) Bttn. "The King's" (Liverpool Regt)

From 1st June 1915.
To 30th June 1915.

Vol II

WAR DIARY or INTELLIGENCE SUMMARY

Army Form C. 2118.

Hour, Date, Place	Summary of Events and Information	Remarks and references to Appendices
1915 1st June RICHEBOURG L'AVOUÉ FRANCE	In trenches — situation quiet but very unsettling — bombardment of by Germans and counter-bombardment. Lieut-Colonel NEALE, commanding officer — wounded by sniper — admitted to field ambulance (2/1 Highland FG) in the evening. Relieved by 2nd BLACK WATCH — relief completed 12 midnight.	1
2nd June RICHEBOURG L'AVOUÉ — LOCRE BERNENCHON	Moved from trenches to LE CORNET MALO (MONT) via crim. RUE DE L'EPINETTE — LE TOURET — LOCON. Arrived about 6 am troubled.	
3rd June LE CORNET MALO	REST BILLET	

Army Form C. 2118.

WAR DIARY
INTELLIGENCE SUMMARY.
(Erase heading not required.)

Instructions regarding War Diaries and Intelligence Summaries are contained in F. S. Regs., Part II. and the Staff Manual respectively. Title pages will be prepared in manuscript.

Place	Date	Hour	Summary of Events and Information	Remarks and references to Appendices
LE CORNET MALO	1915 June 4		Rest billet - Ground heavy.	2
LE CORNET MALO	5		Rest billet - ground hard through. Lt-Col NEALE proceeded on sick leave. Major J.A.C. JOHNSON takes over command (temporary). Extract from the states re Lt-Col NEALE going on sick leave (Authors I.O.C. 154 INF.BDE 407 dated 5/6/15) Major J.J. Smith takes over the duties of Second in Command (temporary) vice Major J.A.C. JOHNSON to be temp. Lt. Col. to continue to command D Coy. from orders received from Brigade to man telegs. Bg	

Army Form C. 2118.

WAR DIARY
or
INTELLIGENCE SUMMARY.
(Erase heading not required.)

Instructions regarding War Diaries and Intelligence Summaries are contained in F. S. Regs., Part II. and the Staff Manual respectively. Title pages will be prepared in manuscript.

Place	Date	Hour	Summary of Events and Information	Remarks and references to Appendices
	1915 June			
LECORNET	6	5.30p	Proceed by road via LOCON - MESPLAUX & LE TOURET.	
MALO	7		Bn billets in Battalion in Brigade Reserve	
LE TOURET		-	Battalion in Brigade Reserve	
			Working parties of 300 men supplied for and a Brigade look by Friends at night	
LE TOURET	8	-	Battalion in Brigade Reserve	
			Working parts supplied for and a Brigade look by French at night	
			Battalion in Brigade Reserve	
LE TOURET	9	8pm	Proceed by road marsh to trenches of Brigade Sect. near Hand GLAGON RUE EAST OF FESTUBERT. Battalion occupies fire and support trenches of Brigade Sect - Battalion Headquarters in reserve trench. 1/4 LOYAL NORTH LANCS REGT occupy what were trenches of Royal Scots. The Battalion relieves 1/4 ROYAL LANCASTER REGT (KINGS OWN) and 1/C SCOTTISH RIFLES refer as fire and support trenches concerned	

Army Form C. 2118.

WAR DIARY
or
INTELLIGENCE SUMMARY.
(Erase heading not required.)

Instructions regarding War Diaries and Intelligence Summaries are contained in F. S. Regs., Part II. and the Staff Manual respectively. Title pages will be prepared in manuscript.

Place	Date	Hour	Summary of Events and Information	Remarks and references to Appendices
LA GORGUE RUE (French)	1915 10.		Situation quiet — working parties at night on communication trenches. Little shell fire. One man accidentally wounded. Leaves Nineteen.	
LA GORGUE RUE (French)	11		Situation quiet — not off afternoon when considerable shrapnel fire from enemy — 2/Lt R H GORDON wounded and a few other ranks wounded. Relieved at night by 2 i/c ROYAL HIGHLANDER & 600 Zouaves trench and moved to PACAUT thro' the billet	
LA GORGUE RUE (French) PACAUT	12			
PACAUT	13..		Colonel Paraid. Captain W.A.S. SHEATH 2nd i/c. Lieut. C. D. HUTCHISON appointed to command 'B' Coy (Reny) vice Capt. SHEATH 2nd i/c with 2/Lt. L. J. DENNIS 2nd in command vice Lt. HUTCHISON. Lt. R. B. J. 146/25 McCarron and Lord Command Officers Resultant — 2nd in Command and Lord Command to Brigade for instruction at Depot attend G.L.8.	

Wt. W10791/1773 500,000 1/15 D. D. & L. A.D.S.S./Forms/C. 2118.

WAR DIARY
INTELLIGENCE SUMMARY

Place	Date	Hour	Summary of Events and Information	Remarks and references to Appendices
	1915. June			
PACAUT	14.	1.30p	Orders of sent march to trench at LE TOURET	
			J.B. Dutton in comm. of attack	
LE TOURET (TRENCHES)	15	—	Battalion in Brigade reserve for attack.	
		6.45p	Orders received to move to support of attacking Battalion — Battalion proceed to FESTUBERT and there collected tools and R.E. stores and carried them to rear of trenches immediately north of LA GUINGUE RUE. — Battalion then occupies fire trench the same the Battalions of Brigade viz — 1/4 "KINGS OWN" (Royal Lancaster Regt) — 1/4 LOYAL NORTH LANCS REGT and 1/6 SCOTTISH RIFLES b/w formed attacks	
LA GUINGUE RUE (Trenches)	16	4.30 a	German trenches. Here the Battalion ultimately suffered to withdraw from enemy trenches — withdrawal completed about 6+7a. and the Battalion held fire trench	
			‡ LIEUT H.C. DOWNES 1/5 the Battn. B.M.G.O. missing.	
		3p	Orders received by C.O. to relinquish 156 Infantry Brigade (Cmdr)	

Army Form C. 2118.

WAR DIARY
INTELLIGENCE SUMMARY
(Erase heading not required.)

Instructions regarding War Diaries and Intelligence Summaries are contained in F. S. Regs., Part II. and the Staff Manual respectively. Title pages will be prepared in manuscript.

Place	Date	Hour	Summary of Events and Information	Remarks and references to Appendices
LA QUINQUE RUE (Festubert)	1915 June 16 (contd)	4 p.m. 4.45 p.m.	to attack German junction EAST of L8. at 6.15 pm. Preliminary bombardment by our artillery commenced. Our infantry attack launched from front trenches NORTH of L8. C Coys — A — B — D in rear as mentioned. Artillery fire so accurate that the rifle & trench mortar (apparently from old German communication trench EAST (8) — machine gun and rifle fire ultimately holding the attack — attempt at bn. to proceed enemy's line.	6
LA QUINQUE RUE (Festubert)	17	a.m.	In pursuance of orders our rifle ceased and on our retirement, a party of the Battalion relieved by 1/3 Kings Own who had occupied trench during the night. The Battalion eventually left trench about 2 a.m. and marched to trenches at LE TOURET — there rested. (6 p.m. Battalion proceed by route march to rest billets at PACAUT WOOD	

Army Form C. 2118.

WAR DIARY
INTELLIGENCE SUMMARY.
(Erase heading not required.)

Place	Date	Hour	Summary of Events and Information	Remarks and references to Appendices
	1915 June			
PACAUT WOOD	18	—	Casualties. 15th 16th 13th ranks 232 (includes officers) The number includes Capt H.M. FINEGAN killed 16 Hunt - 2nd Lieut H.H. DRAKE wounded 16 Hunt died of wounds 15 Hunt - Capt G. BROWN missing 16 Hunt same reported killed - Capt R.P. KEATING wounded 16 Hunt - Capt G. WILLIAMS wounded 16 Hunt not also LIEUT DOWNES missing 15 Hunt (above mentioned) Rest Billets.	
PACAUT WOOD	19	—	REST BILLETS. General HIBBERT DSO GOC 154th Infantry Brigade thanks Battalion for its efforts.	
PACAUT WOOD	20	—	Church Parade.	
PACAUT WOOD	21	11.45pm	Battalion inspected (with ½ Loyal North Lancs Regt in front of Brigade Inspector) by Major-General Barnardiston - Allanson GOC 51st (Highland) Division and thanked by him. Battalion received message through General Allanson from FM Commander Ordel Forbelow from Director Thanks Battalion for its efforts in the attacks 15 & 16 inst.	

Army Form C. 2118.

WAR DIARY
or
~~INTELLIGENCE SUMMARY.~~
(Erase heading not required.)

Place	Date	Hour	Summary of Events and Information	Remarks and references to Appendices
	1915 June			8
PACAUTHOOD	22	3p	Battalion move to W II AC-4 – entry part of HINGES & CANAL (LA BASSÉE CANAL)	
HINGES	23		Working parties of 460 men provided for RE work at trench at night. Working parties provided for RE work at trench. at night.	
HINGES	24	3p	Orders of route march (giving 154 Lyng Argyll) to ESTAIRES (VIA – LOCON – LESTREM – LA GORGUE) and then billet	
ESTAIRES	25	3p	Orders of route march to trench SE of LAVENTIE (VIOLAVENTIE) section D3(part) D6 – E5	
LAVENTIE (Trenches)	26		1st trench – relieving guard – every officer & man rifles in trenches	
LAVENTIE (TRENCHES)	27		10p trench – relieving guard	
LAVENTIE (TRENCHES)	28	9p 10.30p	Relieved by the Royal Eng Regt (KINGS OWN) and march to billet in LAVENTIE – Battalion Royal Reserve. Met. during the day – every company was active and present – little rifle fire – very long affairs of enemy in the trench	

Army Form C. 2118.

WAR DIARY
INTELLIGENCE SUMMARY
(Erase heading not required.)

Place	Date	Hour	Summary of Events and Information	Remarks and references to Appendices
	1915 June			
LAVENTIE	29.		Battalion in Brigade reserve at LAVENTIE	
LAVENTIE	30.		Battalion in Brigade reserve at LAVENTIE	
LAVENTIE	1/7		4th Battn. carried on field	

51st Division

Confidential 121/6292

War Diary

of

1/8 (Irish) Bn. "The King's (Liverpool Regt.)

from
1st July 1915
to
31st July 1915 inclusive

Vol III

WAR DIARY / INTELLIGENCE SUMMARY

Army Form C. 2118.

Original

Place	Date	Hour	Summary of Events and Information	Remarks and references to Appendices
LAVENTIE	Jan 1915 1.		Battalion in Divisional Reserve. Draft arrived from ENGLAND. — Two officers (LIEUTS H.C. MANLEY and F.N.H. BROCKE who enlisted as 2/LIEUTS on joining 1st line units) and 153 men with 3 men (Officers) rejoined on return from BASE.	1
LAVENTIE	2.	8½	Battalion in Divisional Reserve. Went to Services presented by the Battalion.	
LAVENTIE	3.	8½	Battalion in Divisional Reserve.	
		8½	Divisional Field Services not Divisional Reserve — Battalion Church Parade.	
LAVENTIE	4.		Its Church Parade. German shell fired just S.E. of LAVENTIE about 10.4 H.E. shell. Could gain no reason of enemy.	
LAVENTIE	5.	8½	Draft arrived from ENGLAND. LIEUT J. LEIGH & … with Capt F.P.S. MURPHY leaving for England. Pierced with party of 154 INFANTRY. Inspection by G.O.C. Indian Army Corps (Lt-General WILLCOCKS) at 2.30 p.m.	

2½ BRIGADE H.Q. ESTAIRES

WAR DIARY
INTELLIGENCE SUMMARY
(Erase heading not required.)

Army Form C. 2118.

Instructions regarding War Diaries and Intelligence Summaries are contained in F. S. Regs., Part II. and the Staff Manual respectively. Title pages will be prepared in manuscript.

Place	Date	Hour	Summary of Events and Information	Remarks and references to Appendices
	1915 July			21
LAVENTIE	6	8.15	Proceeded with Lieuts. Stephenson & 1/4th Lincolnshire Regt and Lt. Col. [?] Linney Commanding Wiltshire Regt. through [?]	
LAVENTIE	7		Proceeded with parties	
LAVENTIE	8		Proceeded with parties	
LAVENTIE	9	8 a.m.	From R. Tunnels East of PICANTIN (i.e. end of RUE DE TILLELOY) whole Battalion in fire trench — afterwards trench in course of construction eg. Allingh 1/6 Batt ARGYLL and SUTHERLAND HIGHLANDERS (T.F.) from RED LAMP CORNER 20 yds. to right of WORCESTER (?) REDOUBT left (by a point about 50 yards north of crossing No.13 COMMUNICATION trench)	
			Batt. H.Qrs. at POST 18.	
			B.L. Kinsella	
PICANTIN	16		LIST NO. 35. G.H.Q. REWARDS dated 10th July 1915 by Field-Marshal Commander-in-Chief. The following officers of the field staff:—	
			HONOURS and REWARDS. Have authority granted by His Majesty the King to the Field Marshal Commanding-in-Chief the undermentioned Officers, Non-Commissioned Officers and Men	

WAR DIARY

INTELLIGENCE SUMMARY.

(Erase heading not required.)

Army Form C. 2118.

3

Place	Date	Hour	Summary of Events and Information	Remarks and references to Appendices
	1915. July			
PICANTIN	10 contd		have been awarded decoration as shown: THE DISTINGUISHED CONDUCT MEDAL. 1st/8th Battalion, Liverpool Regiment. (T.F.) No. 2321 (acting No 1644) Lance-Corporal P. MAHON. No. 2122 Private J. CUDDE.	
PICANTIN	11		In Trench.	
PICANTIN	12		In Trench.	
PICANTIN	13		In Trench.	
PICANTIN	14		In Trench.	
PICANTIN	15.		In trench. 9th Relieved by 2/5 Lancs Fusiliers. During the 6 days in trench enemy artillery active and every trench mortar nightly 20 - shelling very subject. Casualties by left. Trench mates with our own detachments in trench and paid occasionally Lab used my casualty. On second	

WAR DIARY

Army Form C. 2118.

(Erase heading not required.)

Place	Date	Hour	Summary of Events and Information	Remarks and references to Appendices
PICANTIN	1915 July 15		night quiet to relief partie to Mons and men from 2/5 LANCS FUSILIERS in trenches for instruction	
LE NOUVEAU MONDE	16		Batt'n in Bgd'l Reserve	
LE NOUVEAU MONDE	17		Officers and men worked on fields	
			H'd Qrs in Bgd'l Reserve	
LE NOUVEAU MONDE	18		H'd Qrs in Bgd'l Reserve	
LE NOUVEAU MONDE	19		" " in Bgd'l Reserve	
		11.30	1st Alarm. Batt'n turned out, paraded and marched to Brd'l Alarm Rendezvous and G.O.C. 154 Bgd ordered return to quiet & Batt'n returned to alarm posts. Reported to G.O.C. 154 Bg'd, 35 min from receipt of Alarm in trenches to time Batt'n resumed on pos'n.	
LE NOUVEAU MONDE	20		H'd Qrs in Bgd'l Reserve	

Army Form C. 2118.

WAR DIARY
INTELLIGENCE SUMMARY.
(Erase heading not required.)

Instructions regarding War Diaries and Intelligence Summaries are contained in F. S. Regs., Part II. and the Staff Manual respectively. Title pages will be prepared in manuscript.

Place	Date	Hour	Summary of Events and Information	Remarks and references to Appendices
	1915 July			
LE NOUVEAU MONDE	21		1. Argyll Reserve. C.O. Lieut-Col J.G. CAMPBELL-JOHNSON proceed on leave to ENGLAND 20/7/15	
LE NOUVEAU MONDE	22		1. Argyll Reserve	
LE NOUVEAU MONDE	23		2. Argyll Reserve. 51 (HIGHLAND) Division relieved. 3. Battn proceed by march route to new Billets by NEUF BERQUIN (via ESTAIRES) and then billeted. Whole in Argyll Reserve. Battn supplied working parts during several nights - two teams of machine gun section in trenches with Bucks Yeom relieved Batto on Argyll Reserve. Major J.G. CAMPBELL-JOHNSON together Lieut-Colonel [illeg] Comdr. of Argyll Reserve dated 13 June 1915 (Authority Sd/Intoll at Front Argyll 3/13 July 1915. Supplement dated 15 July 1915) NB [illeg]	
NEUF BERQUIN (near)	24		Battn at rest.	

WAR DIARY

INTELLIGENCE SUMMARY

Army Form C. 2118.

Place	Date	Hour	Summary of Events and Information	Remarks and references to Appendices
	1915 July			6
Neuf Berquin	25		Church Parade.	
Neuf Berquin	26		Batt. at Rest.	
Neuf Berquin	27		Batt. moved to III Army area and remained 7 S/O (Wisernes)	
			DIVISION	
		11.30p	Orders of move went to Bn Coys & in turn. Train with all Batt. incl'd transport leaves La Gorgue and proceed to Corbie disembark of Somme via Berguette - Hazebrouck - St Omer - Calais - Boulogne - Etaples - Abbeville - Amiens	
Corbie	28	1.5p	Amiens Corbie. Departure in 40 minutes — train station 55 minutes and proceed to that transport route to La Neuville — part of Corbie then billet.	
			Group of 10 officers join from Base. Lieut Bodel — Lieut Goodwin — 7/Lieuts Duncan — Woods — Limrick — Mountfield — Hill — Neely — Tunbridge — Toms. Lieuts Bodel and Goodwin send travel 7/Lieuts on (contd)	

WAR DIARY
INTELLIGENCE SUMMARY

Army Form C. 2118.

Place	Date	Hour	Summary of Events and Information	Remarks and references to Appendices
	1915 July			
CORBIE (contd)	28		Duties of Command Officer and M.S.135.	
LA NEUVILLE	29	4.	#5 Command Officer & Asst visited Corbie for instructions as to moving to new front. Command Officer Lieut-Col J.A. Campbell Johnson return from Corbie.	
			Major J.J. Smith proceeds on leave to England	
LA NEUVILLE	30	1.30	Orders to move front via Corbie & Mirecourt to Ribemont (Headqrs) 7 August, Infantry of 154 Inf Bde J.O.G. III Army – Lieut-General Monroe	
		4		
		10.45	Orders of move went from Ribemont via Millencourt to Bouzincourt then billet	
BOUZINCOURT	31	9.15	Proceed via Albert and Aveluy to trenches. Relieve 22nd Regiment d'Infanterie in this sector of occupied 154 Inf Bde & 1st battalion (about 1800 yards). The next to lead of Authuille on south and La Boisselle (in German hands) on South (approximately)	

Army Form C. 2118.

WAR DIARY
INTELLIGENCE SUMMARY.
(Erase heading not required.)

Instructions regarding War Diaries and Intelligence Summaries are contained in F. S. Regs., Part II. and the Staff Manual respectively. Title pages will be prepared in manuscript.

Place	Date	Hour	Summary of Events and Information	Remarks and references to Appendices
BOURNECOURT	1915 July 31 (contd)		Enemy Trench occupied by West extend roughly from J.16 DONNAT to Point C — AVELUT — Ovillers road on South side. Two Coys in 7.1/6 SCOTTISH RIFLES in support — 7/6 LANCS FUSILIERS on left with two coys in 7/16 SCOTTISH RIFLES in support — 1/6 R. LANC. REGT (KING'S OWN) in Royal Reserve at AVELUT. 1/6 N. LANC REGT in Divisional Reserve at MARTINSART. Bryd. Hdqs AVELUT. Tonight the unit at BOUZINCOURT 152 (?) ODE on left, 7.134. ODE, 153 (?) on Rt. E (?) Division on left J St Quinin	

51st Division

121/6692

WAR DIARY

of 1/8 KINGS (LIVERPOOL REGT)

August 1915

Vol IV

WAR DIARY
INTELLIGENCE SUMMARY.
(Erase heading not required.)

Army Form C. 2118.

Place	Date	Hour	Summary of Events and Information	Remarks and references to Appendices
August 1915.				
AVELUY	1		In trenches. Day very quiet although some shelling of trenches and of AVELUY. The trenches are very dry (in chalk and clay) and are of excellent conductivity. Battalion Headquarters situated at POSTE DONNET in clay cut.	
		6 pm.	FRENCH COMMANDANT leaves, although French General retains command of Divisional Sector until 6 am on 2/8/15.	
		9 pm.	Alarm from Trench Artillery that enemy (? WÜRTEMBERGERS) were cutting our offensive f. L.E. DENMAT. All quarters were notified but nothing of any importance ensued.	
AVELUY	2		In trenches.	
AVELUY	3		In trenches.	
AVELUY	4		In trenches. Very little exchange of enemy in these trenches. Few appear to be few and of light calibre (whizz-bangs) which are our heavy guns & considerable amount of artillery support. The entirety of the 18th Division (New Army) contd.	

WAR DIARY
INTELLIGENCE SUMMARY
(Erase heading not required.)

Place	Date	Hour	Summary of Events and Information	Remarks and references to Appendices
	August 1915			
AVELUY (contd)	4	—	Company supplying our Divisional Front	
AVELUY	5	—	½ of trench	
AVELUY	6	—	½ of trench. Battalion of New Army has been working in trenches the last few days (6th BERKSHIRE REGT) with the Unit. This is supposed to be a scheme of 18th Division of training Battalions of New Army in trench warfare by time scale for Europe.	
AVELUY	7	9pm	Relieved in trenches by ½ 1st R. LANC. REGT. and ½ of 8 Coys in trench and "B" Coys in dugout trench below POSTE DONNET. Work done in trench sleep reserve. Men have to go to any trench almost through [illegible] & get rations etc and the country round the front that our detail tests is very big (supposed to be 1800 yards). Teams by chn events. The work to commence today.	

1577. Wt. W.10791/1773 500,000 1/15 D. D. & L.   A.D.S.S./Forms/C. 2118.

Army Form C. 2118.

WAR DIARY
INTELLIGENCE SUMMARY
(Erase heading not required.)

Place	Date	Hour	Summary of Events and Information	Remarks and references to Appendices
	August 1915			3
AVELUY (contd)	7.		Constant rifle and shell at ADELLE at head of BOTTY CALVAIRE below POSTE DONNET so that relief each was to be difficult. Killed at night and men have been buried. Capt. Holgate and the Engineer near to Bryant. Sent Headquarters and the Engineers near to Bryant. Relieved at AVELUY. Relieved 1/2 R LANC REGT there.	
AVELUY	8.		Cloud burst.	
AVELUY	9.		Hostile mortar active in Dzoel Ravine German Avelut and suffer various fires. Also supplies acting, parties to continue construction of stollen on roads to CRUCIFIX CORNER when it is possible. Parts of Argoed Ravine and line in AVELUY could be badly bombarded at any time.	
			At any.	
AVELUY	10.		Works parties as above.	
AVELUY	11.		Works parties as above. 'A' and 'B' Companies large plans attack.	
AVELUY	12.		Works parties as above	
AVELUY	13.		Works parties as above.	

WAR DIARY / INTELLIGENCE SUMMARY

Army Form C. 2118.

Place	Date	Hour	Summary of Events and Information	Remarks and references to Appendices
	August 1915			
AVELUY	14.	2.9p.	Relieved 5/6 SCOTTISH RIFLES and Companies in trenches. Joining the rest of Battn. the whole Battalion proceeded by march route (platoons at intervals) via ALBERT and BOUZINCOURT & SENLIS relieving 2/5 LANCS FUSILIERS than in B Cloud Ravin.	
SENLIS	15		This Battn. is in Divisional Reserve. The headquarters of the 51st (HIGHLAND) DIVISION (our Division) are at SENLIS.	
SENLIS	16		1/5 the Battn supplies working parties to load a reserve line of defence near BOUZINCOURT. — Many employment parties.	
SENLIS	17.		Working parties. Many working parties at SENLIS.	
SENLIS	18.		Working parties. Entrench. Battalion officers & one company of the carried on the new line 600 Entrench. Battalion will an length of SENLIS road of 55 metres. The Battalion seem to carry 7 men at a time hammering up behind line and also of shafts ready to rest to the our line in improvements.	

Army Form C. 2118.

WAR DIARY
INTELLIGENCE SUMMARY.
(Erase heading not required.)

Instructions regarding War Diaries and Intelligence Summaries are contained in F. S. Regs., Part II and the Staff Manual respectively. Title pages will be prepared in manuscript.

Place	Date	Hour	Summary of Events and Information	Remarks and references to Appendices
	August 1915			5
SENLIS	19		Wents Senlis.	
SENLIS	20.		72 Wents Senlis	
SENLIS	21/8/15		to Above	

1577 Wt. W10791/1773 500,000 1/15 D. D. & L. A.D.S.S./Forms/C. 2118.

Army Form C. 2118.

WAR DIARY

INTELLIGENCE SUMMARY.

(Erase heading not required.)

Instructions regarding War Diaries and Intelligence Summaries are contained in F.S. Regs., Part II. and the Staff Manual respectively. Title pages will be prepared in manuscript.

6

Place	Date	Hour	Summary of Events and Information	Remarks and references to Appendices
	August 1915			
SENLIS	21	5.15 a.m	Proceeded by road route (platoons at intervals) via BOUZINCOURT - ALBERT and AVELUY to right sector of trenches at AVELUY fronting occupied by the Munk and took over from 1/4 R LANC REGT and part of 1/8 N. LANC. REGT. 1/4 R LANC REGT in support trenches taken POSTE DONNET & 5/16 Scottish Snipers rather distant at SENLIS.	
AVELUY	22		In trenches. The enemy more active than when the trenches last in these trenches but very unsteady shots of small calibre	
AVELUY	23			
AVELUY	24		In trenches	
AVELUY	25		In trenches	
AVELUY	26		In trenches. Enemy emptying trenches and a crevasse occurred but being the day time the slip clefts every little activity	
AVELUY	27		In trenches	
AVELUY	28		In trenches. In the evening the 1/4 R LANC REGT relieved in support trenches taken POSTE DONNET & Coys of 1/5 LANCS FUSILIERS	

1577 Wt.W10791/1773 500,000 1/15 D.D.&L. A.D.S.S./Forms/C. 2118.

WAR DIARY
INTELLIGENCE SUMMARY
(Erase heading not required.)

Army Form C. 2118.

Place	Date	Hour	Summary of Events and Information	Remarks and references to Appendices
	August 1915			
AVELUY	29		to trench.	
AVELUY	30	No 2 trench.		
AVELUY	31	No 2 trench.	Capt & Staves of 9th (?) New Army with us that in trench and (1/2 of Middlesex Regt & 18th Devons). During first stop they had been employing individual platoon and Coy officers with the 91st in firing trench. Went close in trench. Has been more or less sniping but knowing of BOYAU CENTRALE and outworks of maze trenches at POSTE DONNET commenced. Communicate trench from POSTE DONNET to "A Coys" Leadgate obtained casualties. Lost 2ly in this very hon. suffering knights up in Jan Jany of trench. Other collus without causing much serious loss to man yet.	

JMB

51st Division

Confidential.

121/7049

WAR DIARY

1/8 Kings (Liverpool Regt)

SEPTEMBER 1915

Pat V

P

WAR DIARY
INTELLIGENCE SUMMARY
(Erase heading not required.)

Army Form C. 2118.

September 1915

Place	Date	Hour	Summary of Events and Information	Remarks and references to Appendices
AVELUY	1st Sept 1915		In trenches. Slight shelling by enemy but ample retaliation by our artillery.	1.
AVELUY	2		#3 Coy trenches. Work on trenches in BORGO CENTRALE and materials removed at POSTE BONNET has now been nearly completed.	
		2.30 p	"A" Coy took over "C" Coy's line. "C" Coy's the #3 "D" Coy and "D" Coy's the #4 "A" Coy's.	
AVELUY	3		In trenches. No casualties and usual slight shelling.	
AVELUY	4		In trenches. Brigadier General Wilton & 1st Army Corps Commander visited trenches. Battalion was relieved by King's own at 9.30 pm and Headqrs & MMG Coys went into billets at AVELUY et D Coy remained in reserve dug outs in the Ry down Coy in reserve trench.	
	5		Thanksgiving finding fatigues.	
	6		Usual fatigues & physical Mass attended Am & Evng Rg	

Army Form C. 2118.

WAR DIARY
or
INTELLIGENCE SUMMARY.
(Erase heading not required.)

Place	Date	Hour	Summary of Events and Information	Remarks and references to Appendices
AVELUY	7.	—	Usual fatigue parties. At 8 p.m. C Coy strengthened by 1 platoon B Coy relieved D Coy in firing line. D Coy went into reserve trench at Pt. Donnet but 1 platoon D was attached temporarily to B Coy in AVELUY.	2
AVELUY	8		Usual routine.	
AVELUY	9		Usual routine. One man killed. One man wounded.	
AVELUY	10		Usual routine. German aeroplane brought down near SENLIS.	
AVELUY	11		Battalion moved to MARTINSART into Divisional Reserve at 8 p.m. C & D companies were relieved in the trenches at about 10 p.m. & came straight to MARTINSART.	

Army Form C. 2118.

3

WAR DIARY
INTELLIGENCE SUMMARY.
(Erase heading not required.)

Instructions regarding War Diaries and Intelligence Summaries are contained in F. S. Regs., Part II. and the Staff Manual respectively. Title pages will be prepared in manuscript.

Place	Date	Hour	Summary of Events and Information	Remarks and references to Appendices
	Sept. 1915			
MARTINSART	12.		Church Parade. Small working party provided for R.E. exchange for supply ? party from AUTHUILE.	
MARTINSART	13.		Working party (as above) supplied. Remainder of Battalion occupied in cleaning up and clearing clothing, tickets &c.	
MARTINSART	14.		Working parties (about 250 other ranks in addition to officers)	
MARTINSART	15.	2pm	Battn. marched for Battalion (fouled service cab with pack) via ENGLEBELMER – FORCEVILLE – HEDAUVILLE – BOUZINCOURT – MARTINSART. about 10 mile. Weight considerable. Marched at attention for first hour.	
MARTINSART	16.	2pm	Transport marched out. Tactical scheme. Marched to point N.W. of BOUZINCOURT on BOUZINCOURT – HEDAUVILLE ROAD and practised attack up hill – extended order. Dress – Field service cab with pack.	

1577 Wt.W.10791/1773 500,000 1/15 D. D. & L. A.D.S.S./Forms/C. 2118.

Army Form C. 2118.

WAR DIARY
or
INTELLIGENCE SUMMARY.
(Erase heading not required.)

Place	Date	Hour	Summary of Events and Information	Remarks and references to Appendices
	Sept 1915.			4
MARTINSART	17.		Works parties supplied (2 Officers and about 300 other ranks)	
MARTINSART	18.	9.15 a.m	3rd Battalion Batt. Cornel. Beard via BOIS D'AVELUY to R.I.C. D'ANCRE just west of AUTHUILE.	
		6 p.m	Proceed by route march to trenches at AVELUY to relieve 1/4 R. LANC REGT. and 2 Companies of 1/4 N. LANC REGT. on SECTOR F and relieving 1/4 N. LANC REGT. Owing this met part of 4 officers and 30 other ranks men at Brigade Head School at AVELUY. "1-3/4" Strength "30 Officers and 843 other ranks" (Details of Officers 169 other ranks) left at trenches situation quiet	
AVELUY	19		A. at trenches. Situation quiet.	
AVELUY	20		Proceed to ENGLAND for duty at home. 2/Lieut. H.C. MANLEY. Enemy artillery and rifle fire appears to have increased	

WAR DIARY
INTELLIGENCE SUMMARY

Army Form C. 2118.

Place	Date	Hour	Summary of Events and Information	Remarks and references to Appendices
AVELUY	Sept 1915 21.	—	In trenches. Relieved by 1/8 Argyll & Sutherland Highlanders & 2 platoons of 1/5 Seaforth Highlanders. 154 Infantry Brigade relieved by 152 Infantry Brigade. The Unit march to Millencourt and there billeted. (Unit billets).	
MILLENCOURT	22.		Transport move to Vadencourt Wood. Gentlemen's attire and small part of troops move from Bouzincourt to Millencourt.	
MILLENCOURT	23	8.15 am	Tactical Exercise. March via Lavieville and Bresle to point on Albert–Amiens Road & via road by Ferme St. Laurent and from these proceed to held in enemy supposed to be advancing from Toutencourt via Contay & Vadencourt. Divisional Cyclists and squadron Z Ntd Irish Horse (Divisional Cavalry) has in front of the Unit. Proceed back to via Baizieux and Henencourt.	

WAR DIARY

INTELLIGENCE SUMMARY

Army Form C. 2118.

Place	Date	Hour	Summary of Events and Information	Remarks and references to Appendices
Sept 1915				6
MILLENCOURT	24.		I met Lillith & Cowper Hill.	
		2 pm	Interview from CHEMICAL ADVISER, III ARMY on Gas Instruction. Lynch ste. out on use of tube + ton helmets. All men had a met helmet (adjustive) and moved through a tear filled + Stifling adit gas.	
MILLENCOURT	25.		I met Lillith. Cowper Hill. "Fight" strength 29 officers and 847 other ranks. (Details 4 officers and 119 others)	
			No cloud observed.	
MILLENCOURT	26	5.15 am	Proceeded to trenches at AVELUY and took over sector F. Relieving 1/8 ARGYLL & SUTHERLAND HIGHLANDERS and 2 Platoons of 1/5 SEAFORTH HIGHLANDERS. Quartermaster's Stores and attendant section of Transport moved to BOUZINCOURT. CAPT. L.G.D. HUTCHISON proceeds again 13th (TUNNELLING) Coy. R.E. to detail to transport and is forbid of the Mine at 18/9/15 (vide A.G. - 849. D/385 d. 18/9/15). 2/Lieut. F. ESOBEL assumes command.	

1577 Wt W10791/1773 500,000 1/15 D.D.&L. A.D.S.S./Forms/C. 2118.

WAR DIARY

INTELLIGENCE SUMMARY

Army Form C. 2118.

Place	Date	Hour	Summary of Events and Information	Remarks and references to Appendices
	Sept 1915			5.
AVELUY	27		In trenches. Batt. engaged in sapping on previous occasions in from right to left. A.B, C.D. Coys.	
AVELUY	28		In trenches. Trench improvements carried out in fire trench. Had a trench relief. One trench carried out by Batts in reserve viz. 8th Royal Scots (Pioneer) 8 Batt. 12th Bn. In trenches. German aeroplane brought down between SENLIS and BOUZINCOURT by one of our R Vickers fighter. Maj-General R. BANNATINE-ALLASON, C.B. relinquish command of 51st (Highland) Division 24/9/15 and is succeeded by Maj-General G.M. HARPER C.B. D.S.O. who visited Battery Street this this afternoon. He was accompanied by Brigadier-General HIBBERT and G.S.G.	
AVELUY	29			

LIEUT-COL. IAN STEWART

Army Form C. 2118.

WAR DIARY
INTELLIGENCE SUMMARY

(Erase heading not required.)

Place	Date	Hour	Summary of Events and Information	Remarks and references to Appendices
	Sept 1913			
AVELUY	30		In trenches. Dull weather of late few days which makes them trenches very bad. Began to clear up.	

51st Division

Confidential

121/7551

War Diary

of

1/8TH (IRISH) BATTALION THE KING'S
(L'POOL REGT.)

from 1st October 1915
to 31st October 1915.

Vol VI

1/8th (Irish) Bn "The King's" (L'pool Regt).

Confidential War Diary,
From Oct. 1st to
Oct. 31st 1915.

WAR DIARY
INTELLIGENCE SUMMARY

Army Form C. 2118.

Place	Date	Hour	Summary of Events and Information	Remarks and references to Appendices
AVELUT	Oct. 1915 1	-	2 trenches. Organiser. General G.L. HIBBERT D.S.O. being been evacuated sick, Col. Oley will be visiting left of the trench — the Command of 1/5th of 2 party being 2/5th Dublin Engineers at Lt-Col. HINDLE. Command 1/4 LOYAL NORTH LANCS REGT.	
AVELUT	2	-	2 trenches. GERMAN gun by relief — men shelly 2 our trench then experienced hyphen. (NOTE: by to the evening Headquarters and 2 Companies 1/4 R. LANC REGT have been in support of the Unit at LOWER DONNET and had relieved Command of the Unit. The evening of 2 men to billets in AVELUT. This being taken by one Company 2/5 LANCS FUSILIERS)	
AVELUT	3	-	2 trenches	
AVELUT	4	-	2 trenches	
AVELUT	5	-	2 trenches went forward a skilled	

Army Form C. 2118.

WAR DIARY
INTELLIGENCE SUMMARY.
(Erase heading not required.)

Place	Date	Hour	Summary of Events and Information	Remarks and references to Appendices
	October 1915			
AVELUY	6	-	Inspection.	
AVELUY	7	-	Bde. in trenches. Inspection by Brig. Gen. G.T.G. EDWARDS, C.B. took over command.	
AVELUY	8	-	Bde. in trenches. G.O.C. inspected Bn.	
		a.m.	Relieved by 1/5 Royal Lanc. Regt. Headquarters 4th. Unit and C & D Companies moved to billets in AVELUY. A & B Companies remain in trenches. (One in firing trench, one in LOWER DONNET trench). Lieut-Col. Crichton Command of G.O. 1/5 Royal Lanc. Regt.	
AVELUY	9	-	Bn. in billets.	
AVELUY	10	-	Bn. in billets. Bayonet exercise, class and musketry exercises(?).	
AVELUY	11	-	Bn. in billets. Musketry exercises. R. Sergt - Major and Coys. Sergt - Majors and Coys. Quartermaster Sergts. attend an at B. Hqrs. Kensington.	
AVELUY	12	-	Musketry exercises. Coys. Quartermasters attend BOUZINCOURT. A & B Companies in trenches change places. Bn. in billets.	

Army Form C. 2118.

WAR DIARY
INTELLIGENCE SUMMARY.
(Erase heading not required.)

3

Place	Date	Hour	Summary of Events and Information	Remarks and references to Appendices
	October 1915			
AVELUT	13	—	To Lillie.	
AVELUT	14	—	To Lillie.	
		3.p.	Brigadier sees all Commanding Officers at Brigade Headquarters.	
AVELUT	15	—	To Lillie. This unit take over forward trenches in AVELUT from 2/5 LANC FUSILIERS at front & take the Brigade Reserve from French and join Brigade in	
			A & B Companies come from Lillie.	
AVELUT	16	—	AVELUT in Lillie.	
AVELUT	17	—	To Lillie.	
AVELUT	18	—	To Lillie. Working parties and &c.	
AVELUT	19	—	To Lillie.	
AVELUT	20	—	To Lillie. Working parties supplied to &c. Unit moves the whole in Lillie.	
			Bft'lt Hd'ts in AVELUT send 2 men during the time.	
			B.	

Army Form C. 2118.

WAR DIARY
INTELLIGENCE SUMMARY
(Erase heading not required.)

Instructions regarding War Diaries and Intelligence Summaries are contained in F. S. Regs., Part II. and the Staff Manual respectively. Title pages will be prepared in manuscript.

Place	Date	Hour	Summary of Events and Information	Remarks and references to Appendices
	1915 October			4
AVELUY	21.	2pm	Move to Z Sector (F1 subsect) - Companies in usual portion. The Unit occupies until further orders POSTE BONNET. Headquarters and 2 Companies of 1/4 R. LANC REGT at LOWER BONNET. F1 subsect under tactical command of O.C. the Unit. (Unit relieved in Fire trench of the Unit one 1/4 R.LANC REGT and 2 Companies 1/4 N.LANC REGT.) Relief complete by 3.30 pm.	
AVELUY	22		In trenches.	
AVELUY	23.		In trenches. Casualties: nil. Draft of 50 other ranks report from Base. The missing 4 others returned from hospital, 3 returned from Base. Casualties: missing & wounded - one other rank wounded. LIEUT & QUARTERMASTER H.G. CLARKE leaves for one week's leave to ENGLAND. CAPT. E.M. MURPHY report back from one week's leave to ENGLAND. General: missing & wounded one other rank wounded	

1577 Wt. W.0791/1773 500,000 1/15 D. D. & L. A.D.S.S./Forms/C. 2118.

Army Form C. 2118.

WAR DIARY
INTELLIGENCE SUMMARY
(Erase heading not required.)

Place	Date	Hour	Summary of Events and Information	Remarks and references to Appendices
	Oct. 1915			
AVELUY	24	—	To trenches. Counter-bim: nothing to report. Nil. D.A.D.M.S. of 51st (HIGHLAND) DIVISION visits HQ. Staff. Saw a lot of jolly of men in trenches - suffered with a new outbreak in firing line. Activity stilled in firing line. Very quiet by HQ. Fielding a record of no event.	
AVELUY	25	—	To trenches. The KING James though 51st (HIGHLAND) DIVISIONAL area on visit to troop at the front. Casualties nothing to report. Nil.	
AVELUY	26	—	To trenches. About 10 am Colonel Dalton arrived appeared to the WEST and then away in a move or less westerly direction. Given reason the view that this was a German Captive Colonel Dalton which had been away from it moving but no evidence further of it. (contd.)	

Army Form C. 2118.

WAR DIARY
INTELLIGENCE SUMMARY.
(Erase heading not required.)

Instructions regarding War Diaries and Intelligence Summaries are contained in F. S. Regs., Part II and the Staff Manual respectively. Title pages will be prepared in manuscript.

Place	Date	Hour	Summary of Events and Information	Remarks and references to Appendices
	Oct. 1915			6.
AVELUY	26 (contd)	—	Brigadier-General C.T.G. EDWARDS C.B. (Commander 154 Inf. Bgde.) inspected the billets of Rear Guards (Augusta) & C° Lewis gun & German trench to GILLIERS CEMETERY. 6 Casualties: mostly to Martinsart Rd.	
AVELUY	27	—	Nil. Casualties: mostly to Martinsart Rd.	
AVELUY	28	—	Nil. Cold Front (?) 6" shell bgs. on ground behind LOWER DONNET replaced by R.E. Casualties: mostly to Martinsart Rd. Weather commenced very wet in morning and continued.	
AVELUY	29	—	Nil. About 3.45 a.m. to 9.15 a.m. heavy bombardment of German first position, particularly on our left (by F 2 Batteries) contd.	

BOIS D'AUTHUILE.

WAR DIARY

INTELLIGENCE SUMMARY

Army Form C. 2118.

5.

Place	Date	Hour	Summary of Events and Information	Remarks and references to Appendices
	October 1915			
AVELUY (cont)	29.	—	Casualties: nil other ranks nil. Fine calm day on whole. Field & heavy artillery about THIEPVAL 2pm – 4.30pm Dropped 20 other rank rounds returning fire. About 141 rounds.	
AVELUY	30.	—	"B" & trench.	
		a.m.	Germans put a few shells into AVELUY & ALBERT. Casualties: nil other ranks nil.	
		noon	Germans shell AVELUY & ALBERT about 10 to 12. Midnight and 2 am with trench & incendiary.	
			Shells etc. "B" & trenches.	
AVELUY	31.	—	Casualties: nil other ranks. Two other ranks wounded. All other days were fireworks, on virtually all War Signal of shots in reserve.	

51st Division

Confidential.

121/7636

War Diary

of

1/8TH (IRISH) BATTALION THE KING'S
(L'POOL REGT.)

from 1st to 30th November 1915

Vol VII

WAR DIARY

INTELLIGENCE SUMMARY
(Erase heading not required.)

Army Form C. 2118.

Place	Date	Hour	Summary of Events and Information	Remarks and references to Appendices
AVELUY	November 1915 1	—	In trench. Considerable miles to meals for the cart avoidable wounded. Rain and trench very muddy.	
AVELUY	2	—	In trench. CAPT B SMITH G.F.R. SMITH (RAMC TE) LIEUT G.F.R. SMITH (RAME TE) & H.H. Connolly. Clean SOUVE, LIEUT J.E.MILNE (RAMC) miles, Lifton Scott (Cavalry) Adm: 51st Div B Relieved by 1/4 R. LANC REGT 2nd Suff Co & D Companies in trench.	
AVELUY	3	—	Battalion Headquarters and A & B Companies billetted in AVELUY. 1/2 L. Lillees. Cleaning arms & equipment. Wards, ganta.	
AVELUY	4	—	Brigade fights, camps & clean.	
AVELUY	5	—	LT. COL E.A. FAGAN arrives and is appointed to the Command of the Battalion. (Acting 15 & IB/SC 02 cd 4/11/15)	
AVELUY	6	—	LT-COL F.A. CAMPBELL JOHNSON proceed to ENGLAND. 1/4 (attached) Fd. AM 91 4/11/15 T.Q.C. (Glen quarters) Orts turned out and orders moved from Brigade to return to billets.	

Army Form C. 2118.

WAR DIARY
INTELLIGENCE SUMMARY.
(Erase heading not required.)

Place	Date	Hour	Summary of Events and Information	Remarks and references to Appendices
AVELUY	November 1915			
	April 5. am		154 Infantry Brigade relieved by 152 Infantry Brigade. The Unit was relieved by 2/5 LANCS FUSILIERS & the 1/8 ARGYLL & SUTHERLAND HIGHLANDERS and the Unit moved via ALBERT to MILLENCOURT and the Field- and billets. Brigade Headquarters at HENENCOURT. Quartermaster's Stores move from BOUZINCOURT to MILLENCOURT.	

WAR DIARY
INTELLIGENCE SUMMARY
(Erase heading not required.)

Army Form C. 2118.

3.

Place	Date	Hour	Summary of Events and Information	Remarks and references to Appendices
	November 1915			
MILLENCOURT	8	—	Bn not billets. Men clean arms and equipment. Casualties Nil.	
MILLENCOURT	9	10 am	Commanding Officers funeral. 572 O.R. rank on funeral. The vehicles transport at CONTAY and the [small detach.] Casualties Nil.	
MILLENCOURT	10	10.30 am	Inspection of Battalion by Brigadier-General G.T.G. EDWARDS C.B (Commanding 154th Infantry Brigade) 543 O.R. rank on funeral (the vehicles transport at CONTAY and the small detach). Practice attack on trenches outside village — Brigadier General 2/Lt J.N.H. BROOKS rejoin Bn from leave (expired). Casualties nil. to night Nil.	
MILLENCOURT	10	—	Bn Coy Training. Casualties Nil.	
			Bn Field Firing M. Casualties Nil.	
MILLENCOURT	12	—	Coy Training. Casualties Nil.	
MILLENCOURT	13	—	Draft of one officer (2/Lt L.J. DENNIS) and 31 O.R. rank (= 28 from ENGLAND and 3 rejoining from base) arrive. Kit inspection. Casualties Nil.	
MILLENCOURT	14	—	Church Parade. Snow at night.	

WAR DIARY

INTELLIGENCE SUMMARY

Army Form C. 2118.

Place	Date	Hour	Summary of Events and Information	Remarks and references to Appendices
MILLENCOURT	November 1915			4.
	15	7am	Physical Training & Squad Drill.	
		9.30 am	Batt. Parade. Church Parade. Lecture on No. 19.3. ("Battery work 3 inch mortar & Lewis gun") by Private SUMNER, H.T.D.S. Promoted 2 yrs 2nd Lieut. Whilst in intelligence did not afternoon. Conf. Trench digging in a swamp. Other pers. Highland unit - off to midst of the same at night. Casualties: mildly to midst of the same at night.	
MILLENCOURT	16	12	Batt. paraded & proceeded to route march to trenches via ALBERT-AVELUY-AUTHUILLE. G.2 relieved AUTHUILLE via ALBERT-AVELUY-AUTHUILLE. Relieve 1/6 ROYAL HIGHLANDERS (BLACK WATCH) (154 Infantry Brigade) relieves 153 Infantry Brigade.) G.1 relieved a Coy. new half of 1/6 SCOTTISH RIFLES 1/4 ROYAL LANC. REGT. - G.3 relieved a Coy of 2/5 LANCS FUSILIERS. G.4. Disposition (from right) A. - C. - D. Companies in firing trench - B Coy in support. Casualties: mildly to midst. Nil.	

Draft of 2/Lt. R.H. GORDON rejoins Unit from England. [3 nm]

1577 Wt.W.12791/1773 500,000 1/15 D.D.&L. A.D.S.S./Forms/C. 2118.

Army Form C. 2118.

WAR DIARY
INTELLIGENCE SUMMARY.
(Erase heading not required.)

Instructions regarding War Diaries and Intelligence Summaries are contained in F.S. Regs., Part II. and the Staff Manual respectively. Title pages will be prepared in manuscript.

Place	Date	Hour	Summary of Events and Information	Remarks and references to Appendices
	November 1915			5.
MILLENCOURT (contd)	16	—	(cancelled) & Doie.	
			2/Lt G.L.H. FISHER rejoins Unit from Machine Gun Course at WISQUES. Guntonels and MARTINSART.	
AUTHUILE	17	—	12 L trunks.	
			Fine trench about 100 yards long - had regained Pack trench by T.enemy trench mortar which we rather active. Burnt this subsect. 2-5 guns 2/LTEP.LOUR had 98 dugouts will with about 2.5 other Casualties. Orders to massage to send runners.	
			12 L trunks. 2/LTERLOUP.	
AUTHUILE	18	—	Brigadier General EDWARDS (GOC 154 Infantry Bgde) inspected trenches. Casualties missed turnels 4 athenal runnels. Had a new artillery etc. Liveness.	
			12 L trunks	
AUTHUILE	19.	—	More trench mortar activity on front of enemy. Test of green rocket signal - threw at a time. (contd)	12

Army Form C. 2118.

WAR DIARY

~~INTELLIGENCE SUMMARY.~~

(Erase heading not required.)

Remarks and references to Appendices
6.

Place	Date	Hour	Summary of Events and Information	Remarks
AUTHUILE (contd)	November 1915 19.		repeated twice at 30 second interval. This signal means our artillery fires short & to shorten range. Lt Col. Jewell & 2nd in Comd Capt. Oxford Hampshire recommend our Ofr trenches. It was in trenches could live and afford lights and as the trench is found. Casualties midday to midnight Nil.	
AUTHUILE	20.	10 PM 1T	2 shrapnel. Artillery (own) carried out an evening silence. Quiet enemy. Casualties midday to midday one other rank wounded. 1/L (Two officers Lts. Lt Brangl reconnaissance Lt 2nd Lts of Hampshire - A. O'Connor)	
AUTHUILE	21.		2 shrapnel. Casualties midday to midday one other rank killed 1/L rifle bullet.	

WAR DIARY

INTELLIGENCE SUMMARY

(Erase heading not required.)

Place	Date	Hour	Summary of Events and Information	Remarks and references to Appendices
AUTHUILE	November 1915 22	—	In trenches.	2
		a.m.	G.O.C. (Lt-Col L. STEWART-M) in trenches. Casualties nil. Relief to night by 1/2 N. Lancs. Regt. relieve 1/4 R. Lancs Regt in relief moving out at 9 p.m.	
		—	1/4 N. LANCS. REGT relieve 1/4 R. LANC REGT in G.1. trenches	
		11.30 p.m.	Battalion to Brigade reserve AUTHUILE	
AUTHUILE	23	—	In trenches.	
		a.m.	Brigadier visits trenches. Chevallier relief to nailing the old road killed. Two other ranks wounded.	
		6.30 a.m.	Trench mortar shell fell in SAUCHIE HALL STR. Guide to relief Today relief 4 casualties. Some trench mortar shells and "coal can" fired 5 enemy.	
		8.30 p.m.	Trench mortars (from 1/4 R. LANC REGT) and 2 Bryant & Listers 4 rounds of toffee apples reply that enemy (crump)	

WAR DIARY

INTELLIGENCE SUMMARY

Army Form C. 2118.

Place	Date	Hour	Summary of Events and Information	Remarks and references to Appendices
AUTHUILE	November 23 1915 (cont)	—	are mining and have reached point below our fire trench immediately south of THIEPVAL SOUTH POINT and of Listening Post 52C. Listening Sap 25. Subsequent to an offensive from 139 K (TUNNELLING Co?) R.E. mile wire system being cut night and morn. Capt. I.E. JACKSON D.S.O. 6COS visit to Field Ambulance. Reports no mines.	
AUTHUILE	24	—	12 of tunnels.	
		11am	Fire extreme spent enemy our trench mortar Kensington etc. to make them slacken their mortar firing etc. — great shoots. Casualties midday to midnight. One of our Batteries shelled.	
AUTHUILE	25	—	Patrols	
		12m	Practice alarm and annoying attack on Thiepval South Point (SALIENT) with bombers - carrying parties etc.	[Envs]

WAR DIARY / INTELLIGENCE SUMMARY

Army Form C. 2118.

Place	Date	Hour	Summary of Events and Information	Remarks and references to Appendices
Neuville	November 1915			
AUTHUILE	25	9.24 p.m (circa)	Cracker alarm from Aveluy — Conspicuous turmoil out. Very quickly saw close shellfire (shells). Showed nothing further (shellfire). Casualties — nil to enemy. MG trench.	Promulgation of F.G.C.M. on 24/11/15. No. 2691 Private M. O'CONNOR. Charged with "when on active service disobeying a lawful command given by his superior officer." Sentenced to 56 days F.P. No. 1. Signed W.M.?
AUTHUILE	26	—	Various bursts of enemy MG fire in trenches this evening. Have neglected many from this unit and reports received of no movement. At shell wrecked ambush ascertained no advance nil for our defence.	
		10 am	Fire scheme — (our trench mortar — machine gun — West trench them — rifle grenades — Jedinall and howitzer) to treat enemy over a bridge on his attempt to renew it to enable them by 26/25. — Doesn't wind at cattle to our own myth. Casualties nil to enemy Nil.	

WAR DIARY
INTELLIGENCE SUMMARY

Army Form C. 2118.

10.

Place	Date	Hour	Summary of Events and Information	Remarks and references to Appendices
	November 1915			
AUTHUILE	27	—	In trenches.	
			Lt-Col. E.A. FAGAN proceeds on leave to England — MAJOR J.J. SMITH in command. Casualties. Night & midday one other rank wounded.	
AUTHUILE	28	—	In trenches. Heavy Enemy shelling during night. (more than usual) Trenches much damaged. Much nil.	
		6 p.m.	Relief commenced by 1/6 ARGYLL & SUTHERLAND HIGHLANDERS of the Unit in G.2 sector.	
		8.17 p.m.	Completed. The unit proceeded to MILLENCOURT. The billets (15th Hqrs Bgd) relieved 152 Bgd Argyll in G sector and grew more tired to Divisional reserve.	
MILLENCOURT	29	11.35 p.m.	Battalion billeted in MILLENCOURT.	
		—	In and billets. Complete midday & night kit. H.O. Cleaning up and clothing and refitting of uniform.	

Army Form C. 2118.

WAR DIARY
INTELLIGENCE SUMMARY.
(Erase heading not required.)

Instructions regarding War Diaries and Intelligence Summaries are contained in F. S. Regs., Part II. and the Staff Manual respectively. Title pages will be prepared in manuscript.

Place	Date	Hour	Summary of Events and Information	Remarks and references to Appendices
MILLENCOURT	November 1915 30	— 10 am	First letter. Batt. Parade inspection. Batt. Amb. School commenced. Committee meeting to decide XVd.	

Confidential

WAR DIARY

of

1/8TH (IRISH) BATTALION THE KING'S
(L'POOL REGT.)

from 1st December 1915 to 31st December 1915

Vol VIII

WAR DIARY
INTELLIGENCE SUMMARY

Army Form C. 2118.

Place	Date	Hour	Summary of Events and Information	Remarks and references to Appendices
	December 1915			1
MILLENCOURT	1	—	Inset billets.	
		5.30 a.m.	Opened reveries — running — Bayonet exercises.	
			Coys Trains — extended fire - extended order	
		10—	drill. Synthetic visits guards.	
			Gents Clan.	
			Cavalries miles to miles Bat.	
			Detachment of 13 L.H.L.L. billets in valley at foot	
			of Division who are probably relieving our Division	
			(51st) This being 32nd Division (?)	
	LT MAHON		Leaves of Asquith's name relief 1st NORFOLKS	
MILLENCOURT	2	—	In not billets.	
			Warlies parties.	
			Cavalries miles to miles Bat.	
MILLENCOURT	3	—	In not billets.	
		5.30 a.m.	Opened reveries	
			Cayo Traini	2.30 — Composite Football
				Match 2/5 LANCS
				FUSILIERS at
				MARTINSART-game
		10 a.m.	Cavalries miles to miles to meet memory	in Division Rugs.
			Cavalries miles to meet memory	

WAR DIARY
INTELLIGENCE SUMMARY.
(Erase heading not required.)

Army Form C. 2118.

Place	Date	Hour	Summary of Events and Information	Remarks and references to Appendices
MILLENCOURT	March 1915 4	—	2nd Wilts. Went to trenches. Casualties: under. One all round casualty (2 O/R) wounded & sent to hospital. M.G. not used.	2/
MILLENCOURT	5	12 pm	Batt. moves to trenches via ALBERT and AVELUY (Arr at 3.30 pm). F₂ subsect. — A Coy from extreme right P123 to junction of WHALLEY STREET & fire trench — D Coy from left of A's to junction of FURNESS STREET & fire trench — B's from right of D's to P133 — rest of fire trench held by 1/4 R. LANE REGT (3 Coys in). Coy & machine gun in line from P123 to P133. — Headqrs of the Battn. at POSTE DONNET. One Coy of 1/4 R. LANE RESERVE in LOWER DONNET (4 Coys), Hdqrs of 1/4 R. LANE RESERVE LOWER DONNET with one section Engineers in support (one).	

WAR DIARY

INTELLIGENCE SUMMARY

Army Form C. 2118.

Place	Date	Hour	Summary of Events and Information	Remarks and references to Appendices
MILLENCOURT.	December 1915. 5 (contd)	—	OC submits Lt Col E.A FAGAN (Gen¹⁵) Lt relinquishes from Lt Col CARLETON 1/6 R LANC REGT) Trench recently had entire — meeting why casualties moved to mules nil. Troops relieved. 1/5 GORDONS with one Coy 1/5 GORDONS in firing line and 2 Companies 1/6 BLACK WATCH at LOWER BONNET. Relief complete 5.30 pm (1/5 3rd Hy Bde relieved 1/5 Hy Bde- 405 AVELUY) Guards move to BOUZINCOURT. Relief	
AVELUY	6	—	of Reserve Coy. miles to miles nil. Lt Col FAGAN returns from leave assumes command of Battalion. Three Companies I 1/4 R LANC REGT & Hd Qrs of Battalion relieved by A & B Companies 13th L.F. in instructions	

WAR DIARY
INTELLIGENCE SUMMARY

Army Form C. 2118.

Place	Date	Hour	Summary of Events and Information	Remarks and references to Appendices
AVELUY	December 1915 7	-	2 funerals. Weather fine.	
AVELUY	8	-	B.2 Trench. Casualties: 1 wounded, 1 missing Bn.	
		7pm	Co. D Company 13 A.H.L.I. took over right half of sector line - a relief A.B.D. Companies of this Unit proceed to Aveluy where 2 sections of Beauvelin Jcn.	
			Headqrs 13 H.L.I. occupy POSTE BONNET Headqrs 8th Unit occupy LOWER BONNET W.Col sabrect till took command of Lt. Col E.A. F.A.G.A.N. Casualties: 1 wounded, 1 missing Bn.	
AVELUY	9	-	B. 2 Trench.	
		7pm	Went South. Handed to Companies in Aveluy. Casualties: killed 1 wounded Bn. LT. COL R.S. O'DELL commanding 3rd H.L.I. (Special Reserve) is 7th June England.	

WAR DIARY
INTELLIGENCE SUMMARY
(Erase heading not required.)

Army Form C. 2118.

Place	Date	Hour	Summary of Events and Information	Remarks and references to Appendices
AVELUY	Dec 1915			5.
AVELUY	10	-	Lt Col O'Dell commanding 3rd H.L.I. left this unit.	
	11	-	Trenches. Lieutenia — holiday pour. 2nd Lieut Donelly & 2nd Lieut Luswick left for 3rd Army course duration about 1 month. (General instruction). C & D Companies 17th H.L.I. relieved by our A & C Companies. Our B relieved our C at Laun DONNET B Coy stayed in AVELUY	
	12	-	In Trenches. Working parties found by Companies in support in AVELUY.	
	13	"	In Trenches. Usual working parties found.	
	14	"	In trenches. A Coy relieved by D. D relieved by B in supports & A took over billets from B in AVELUY.	
	15	"	In trenches. Usual working parties.	
	16	"	The battalion was relieved by the 6th Argyles in firing line & by 1/6th Seaforths in supports. Battalion went into billets in MILLENCOURT.	

Army Form C. 2118.

WAR DIARY
INTELLIGENCE SUMMARY.
(Erase heading not required.)

6

Place	Date	Hour	Summary of Events and Information	Remarks and references to Appendices
	December 1915			
MILLENCOURT	17		In billets. rest & clean up.	
"	18		In billets. working party of 1 Officer & 50 men. Company training	
"	19		In billets. Church parade & working party 1 Officer & 50 O/R.	
"	20		In billets. Battalion inspection strict, usual working party found.	
HÉBUTERNE	21		This Battalion relieved the 6th Black Watch & took over in trenches 92 subsection A.B.D. Coys in firing line & C coy in support	
	22		In trenches. No casualties. Bn on left of 7½ Lancashire Fusiliers on right. 1 Scottish Rifles	
	23		In trenches. no casualties.	
	24		In trenches. no casualties.	
	25		In trenches. no casualties.	
	26		In trenches. no casualties – group of 4 & 6. O.R. went down for some 7½	
	27		In trenches. no casualties	
	28		In trenches. no casualties.	
	29		In trenches. no casualties. Lieut Col Berry of 1st 9th City of London	
	30		In trenches. are Brigadier attached for instruction. Bn Queen Victoria Rifles	

Army Form C. 2118.

WAR DIARY
or
INTELLIGENCE SUMMARY.
(Erase heading not required.)

Place	Date	Hour	Summary of Events and Information	Remarks and references to Appendices
Givenchy	1915			5
Artillerie	31		In trenches. No casualties	

EB Fagan Lt-Col
Comdg 1/8 Kings (Liverpool Regt)

www.ingramcontent.com/pod-product-compliance
Lightning Source LLC
Chambersburg PA
CBHW081445160426
43193CB00013B/2386